TELL ME LIES

by

POEMS 2005-2008

ADRIAN MITCHELL

Pictures
by
Ralph STEADman

A POET-TIC

BLOODAXE BOOKS

ISBN: 978 1 85224 843 7

First published 2009 by
Bloodaxe Books Ltd,
Highgreen,
Tarset,
Northumberland NE48 1RP.

www.bloodaxebooks.com
For further information about Bloodaxe titles
please visit our website or write to
the above address for a catalogue.

Bloodaxe Books Ltd and Adrian Mitchell
acknowledge the financial assistance
of Arts Council England.

Printed in Great Britain by
Bell & Bain Limited, Glasgow, Scotland.

DEDICATION.

*for all my family
and friends
and for all peacemakers*

ACKNOWLEDGEMENTS

Some of these poems have been broadcast by BBC Radio 4 and on BBC1's *Andrew Marr Show*. Some have been performed for the Campaign for Nuclear Disarmament, the Stop the War Coalition, The Medical Foundation for the Victims of Torture, as well as in theatres, schools, pubs, colleges, clubs and festivals in St Andrews, Lewes, London, Aldeburgh and Shetland. Many others were published in *Red Pepper* magazine which gave me the proud title of The Shadow Poet Laureate.

The translation from Brecht, 'About the Child Murderer Marie Farrar', and my own 'The Baby on the Pavement', were commissioned by Poetry International, first performed at the Royal Festival Hall in London and published in *Modern Poetry in Translation*. 'West End Blues' was commissioned by Carol Ann Duffy for an anthology of musical poems, and 'Sad Walk' was commissioned and first published by *Sirena* magazine. 'The Song of the Cross of St Projet' was inspired by the drawing by John Furnival which accompanies it here. 'Death Is Smaller Than I Thought' was read on video and published in the DVD-book *In Person: 30 Poets*, edited by Neil Astley, filmed by Pamela Robertson-Pearce (Bloodaxe Books, 2008).

Many thanks are due to Arts Council England for a Writers' Award which helped my work on this book and others.

EDUCATIONAL HEALTH AND SAFETY WARNING

None of the work in this or any other of my books or plays is to be used in connection with any examination or test whatsoever. If you like a poem of mine, learn it, recite it, sing it or dance it – wherever you happen to be. But don't force anyone to study it or vivisect it or write a well-planned and tedious essay about it. This is the first step in The Shadow Poet Laureate's scheme to destroy the examination systems of the world, which have made true education almost impossible. Free the teachers and the children!

The Shadow reminds all students who are not happy that no law compels them to attend school – so long as it can be proved that they are being educated satisfactorily. (Contact Education Otherwise for information and help.) It is very hard for teachers and children to be happy in overcrowded schools. The Shadow would ask you to consider the ideal size for a school class. Most teachers agree with me that it would be about twelve. Even Jesus couldn't manage thirteen.

CONTENTS

ENJOY THE LIGHT
Love, friendship and sheep

A WALK ON THE WEIRD SIDE
or *Better Out Than In*

Words cry out for pictures...

I glory in the brave work of Ralph Steadman, and am very happy
he has lent me some of his pictures for the cover and interior of
this book, to stand alongside my poems, and has also inscribed
their titles in his own magical hand.

Purists say that poems should stand alone on the page. My poems
know they could stand alone, but don't see why they should have
to. Sometimes it's great if they can be set by a composer like Mike
Westbrook or Richard Peaslee or Andrew Dickson or Pete Moser
and sung by old jazz singers or young rockers. They want to jump
about, not lie on the page like corpses on a slab.

Once I gave a series of about seventy very short lectures in Swan-
sea called *Who Killed Dylan Thomas?* I asked Ralph to lend me
his portrait of Dylan for the cover, so he asked for a look at the
lectures. A month later he sent the pages back, with drawings of
Dylan in various guises on every page. It was a joy then and now
for my thoughts and poems to dance together with the drawings
of one of the greatest draughtsmen of our time and my very dear
friend, the wild wizard Ralph Steadman.

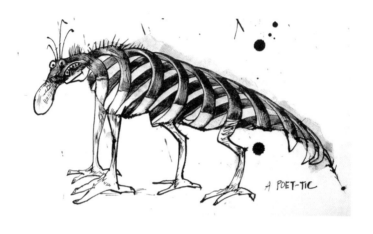

A POET-TIC

APOLOGY IN ADVANCE

ANYTHING THAT MAY CAUSE OFFENCE
PUT IT DOWN TO MY YOUTH AND IGNORANCE

OH

RIVERS RUN THROUGH IT

OR WATERWORKING

16

RIVER NOTES

a river needs banks
    thanks
but the point of a river
  is the river
that walking water

    *

a play in prose
or a play in verse?
a journey by canal
   or down a river?

      *

somebody in a small blue boat
     travelling along
   the heartbeat of the river
   only the river knows who

      *

dirty the river
dirty your mother

      *

   early morning
the riverbank willows
  breathing mistily
and the birds sing
their high and watery songs

      *

in the river mud
  sinking slowly
old wrist-watches

      *

I'm going to the seaside.
    me too.
   two rivers meet
   and join together

WEST END BLUES

(a river trip)

West End Blues was recorded by Louis Armstrong and his Hot Five
in 1928. Louis played cornet, Fred Robinson was on trombone,
Johnny Dodds played clarinet and Earl Hines was the pianist.
These verses follow, more or less, their improvisations that day.
But their subject is not the responsibility of Louis and the Hot Five.
It was inspired by a holiday at Tom and Sally Vernon's house in the
Cévennes in 2007, when my wife Celia and I spent several happy weeks
in the river Hérault at the bottom of their garden with our Golden
Retriever, Daisy the Dog of Peace.

CORNET

Louis Armstrong
picked up the sun
and blew it
with all of the gold
in his wonderful thunderful heart

then he blew a little tighter
till the sun was double brighter
playing a song together
said we belong together
      shine
saying that soon you'll be mine

Come along
come along to the river
let's go on down
The rivers a real wonderway
birds and fishes
let's go on down
and sit together there
on the sweet riverbed
let's go on down
to that sweet riverbed
we'll lie till dawn
in the cool clear water
and name all the stars in the sky

TROMBONE

Long way
to walk
I'm tired
maybe I won't find my way to
that old river
But I want to go down
Yes I want to go meet you
I'll be coming
someday I'll join you
at the water way down there

CLARINET

waterbird
swooping low
dragonflies
all aglow

butterflies
   fluttering
little fish
   flickering

river's my home
river's my home
      yes
river's my home

SCAT SINGING BY SATCHMO

sunny skies
breezy and blue
and April air
for me an' you

the tall trees are swaying
they dance with the stream
         little clouds drifting
            free as a dream

river's my home
river's my home
      yes
river's my home

PIANO

pebbles rolling underneath our toes
eddies running round in spirals
down where the boulders form a dam

come and take my hand
come and walk along the dam
and we'll dive
in the swimming hole
while all the dogs stand staring
at you and me
down on the riverbank
they wag their tails at us
laughing in the swimming hole

CORNET

Here we are...

    now we're river walking
      down the river
          river walking
     through the country
splashing down the river
      to a little boat
    a small green boat

    Let's climb aboard
     and sail away
    right out to sea

PIANO

on board
  set sail
and out
  to sea
    yes

CORNET

Now we'll have our dinner
  and then go to bed.

20

FIVE WALKS

I was asked to write a poem to the beautiful music of Chet Baker's
Sad Walk by the magazine *Sirena*. First I wrote a poem called *Sad Walk*,
about a morning when I walked my dog a few hours after hearing the news
of the death of my adopted daughter and the world seemed cold and grey.

I wrote it so that the words fit some of Chet Baker's solos, but not
exactly. But then I thought that the music of *Sad Walk* isn't simply sad.
It has a beauty to fit any mood. So I wrote a cheerful poem on a similar
pattern and called it *Glad Walk*. Then a child's bad dream poem called
Bad Walk. Then, remembering my father at the seaside – *Dad Walk*.
And finally, since nonsense makes sense to me, *Mad Walk*.

SAD WALK

down a dark purple
    tarmac path
        under a sky
full of ashes and smoke

  broken-down trees
     pale yellow moon
  near the edge of the world
      on the edge

  now the heart is grey
     even grass is grey
  and the city traffic
keeps screaming and screaming
     where have you gone?

  down a dark purple
     tarmac path...

GLAD WALK

walk up the silver
   tower stairs
   into a sky
of a zillion stars

zebras may graze
   friendly giraffes
take their ease in the light
   of the moon

as my eyes delight
   in the singing grass
and the flying foxes
   are diving and soaring
I take your hand

walk up the silver
   tower stairs...

over the high wall's
　　razor wire
plunge to a moat
　　where the crocodiles lurk

stumble through thorns
　　into the swamp
till you feel yourself sink
　　　into dark

　　　as you gasp your last
　　you are grasped and raised
　　　back into the air by
　　the hand of an ogre
who laughs and throws you

　　　over the high wall's
　　　razor wire...

DAD WALK

lie by a rockpool
watch the green
  hair of seaweed
and the flickering fish

  climb up a rock
    big as a house
you can almost see France
    from the top

  we will dam the stream
  running down the beach
  till we've formed a salt lake
  so deep we'll swim and then
    flood mum's deckchair

  lie by a rockpool
  watch the green…

MAD WALK

roundabout backwards
   songs of cheese
   chanted through teeth
of potatohead spooks

   accelerate
   past logic bog
pay the beggars of time
   with an owl

   safari me out
for the glue's in flower
and the nightmare police
are all kens and barbies
   marching in flames

roundabout backwards
   songs of cheese...

An Erik Satie Breeze Blows Through Honfleur

(for John and Astrid Furnival)

    silver moth tables
      round the harbour
        small waves wavering
          watched by the yellow eyes
            by a prowling, jet-black cat
        we sip our coffees
     a chair blows over – bam!
        Satie.

you stand with your back to
   the battered old green doors
     leading to the garden
       of the magical composer's house
         the chained doors behind you
      suddenly shove
   and try to burst open – bang!
        Satie.

    the sun is big
    the sun is strong enough
  to lift the stone and water town
   with its restaurants, its museums
and its glorious double-decker carousel
   way up into the sky

and now my saffron serviette
   bounces out of my lap
     and up and off
     over the tourists and the dog-walkers
     ten minutes later
   I see it somersaulting
round and round a traffic roundbout – phuish!
     Satie.

CITY SONGS

FEDERICO GARCIA LORCA

RALPH STEADman 2003

or DON'T MUTTER IN THE GUTTER

NOTHING FEELS AS GOOD AS GOLD.

(slogan on jeweller's shop in Kentish Town)

gold's hard shine
    hurts my eyes
which love the gentle
blue and white of speedwell

all the gold I ever owned
was in a fat gold watch
which somebody left me
and some ghost stole –
(but I can still tell the time) –

or in the wedding ring
which jumped off my finger
as I climbed a tree
and was never found again –
(nor was the marriage);

    strap a watch on your wrist
which says ten thousand pounds
        and the time's ripe
      for you to get mugged
      by some junkie mother
    who never had anything
    but needs, bleeds, greeds,
killer cigarettes and murderous debts.

    all gold is fool's gold.
out of the lying grounds of the world
    up comes the gold
grinning like a murderer.

THE MEANING OF MY LIFE

Having looked at my life, comparing it with the lives of the people in soaps and the newspaper columnists and the people in magazines and the people in romantic fiction, I failed to discover any colour or meaning in it.

So I bought the latest mobile and compiled a list of 100 friends and near-friends and relations whom I could call and entered their numbers.

Now I phone them at random – number 34 – and tell her about My Day – how I went shopping this morning (O, what did you buy?) about the rude shop assistant who commented on my weight (the cheek of it!) and the Italian boy in the boutique (Aaaah!). And the bus which didn't stop for me and the bus that did, and choosing the right marge and spaghetti and what my Mother said on the phone last night (No!) and what number 78 said this morning (Well, I'd delete her!) and gradually My Day passes (And so, what are you doing tonight?) watching Corrie and The Bill probably and gradually, between what I report and what my numbers comment on what I report, and what my friends report and what I comment on what my numbers report, the meaning of my life begins to emerge, like lumps of fluff from under the bed.

BUDAPEST MAY 2008

if I press the little brass lever
that unlocks my hotel room door
and look out into the corridor
will I be able to lock the door
if I don't like what I see outside?

if I could find a photograph
of all the people in Budapest
walking through the streets
from 1939 to 2008
and magnify that photograph
and then animate it
I could see who is dead and who is alive
because the dead ones
would stop in their tracks
and the live ones
would keep on walking

there were many other dreams
but like little dark curls
they have gone down
the plughole of the morning

crawler potato autogate

those words broke out of my head
like a baby ostrich from its shell
words that have never before
been connected in one line of poetry or prose
   Originality!
I have found it at last
   by digging in to the rich soil of the
crawler potato autogate
    field
in my own head
   that dreamfield

   Originality fans look out –
   here comes another one!

    owl targoals baited!

Wake up, Adrian –
I'm not going to clean up the mess
left by your bloody ostrich!

We go out shopping
I see ragged red roses
     in a rag rug
made in nowhere

In the local dreamshop
a very foreign voice says:
'the dog's disjointed wound
     is been and gone.'
I buy exactly nothing.

Back in the hotel
I can hear forty waterfalls
constantly flowing down
inside the walls of our room.

Oh...I found my red glasses!
Shall we go for a walk round the island?

The Milk Float

the dark cars
still as statues
at four A.M.

between them glides
and swerves to the pavement
the blue-white ghost craft of the streets

it stops with an elongated squeak
then the jangle of a construction kit
made up of triangles and rhombuses

then the warm whine of starting up again
and the light mother ship departs
leaving us cardboard orange juice trees
and little glassy breasts of milk

The Baby on the Pavement

People keep telling me about Human Nature
and how vile it is.
I have made up this story for them:

There is a naked baby
lying on the pavement.

No, the naked baby
is lying on a blanket
on the pavement.
(I find I can't leave it there
without a blanket,
even in a story.)

Watch the first human being
who comes walking down the pavement.

Does he step over the baby and walk on?
Does he kick the baby and walk on?

He picks up the baby,
wraps it in the blanket
and tries to find somebody
to help him look after the baby.

Isn't that your Human Nature?

'Nobody can tell me what
they are meant to be for!'
Cried the suburban lady
As she poured a cardboard box full of garden snails
Into the dusty gutter.
Then she marched up and down the gutter
cracking their shells open with her heels,
Stamping the snails to death with her boots.

It was an ugly thing to do.

Nobody can tell me what
the suburban lady is meant to be for.

MORE FRIENDS

One friend refused a title
One took a bad black pill
One friend wept her heart out
Another one forged his will

I send my wildest wishes
To each and every friend
I'll keep washing up the dishes
As my train rolls round the bend

I could have been with you much more
But work stole all my time
And I hurt many I am sure
By neglect, that shoddy crime.

I drank a bottle of Dylan
A powerful Celtic blend
It brought out my hero and villain
And it rolled me round the bend

Some friends they say *Take Care* to me
I answer *Take a Chance*
They say *Revolutions always fail*
I ask *What happened to France?*

Buy yourself a seat in the House of Pretence
Find the number in the Yellow Pages
Rent Arthur's Round Table for your Conference
Welcome to the Middle Ages

We're going to have another Old Etonian
As her majesty's PM
While New Labour melts into a pool
Of ineffectual intellectual phlegm

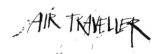

AIR TRAVELLER

up the aisle
and down the aisle
of the shivering aeroplane
pads the two-year-old boy
with huge brown eyes

he waves solemnly
to the people
on each side of the aisle
of the shivering aeroplane

everyone
even the whingey
seven-year-old boy
waves back

THE DIRTY SMOKERS

Beyond the golden portals of the Otis lifts
Beyond the atrium's marbleised floors
Beyond stolid Security
Beyond languid Reception
You stand in huddles, out of doors

You are the Dirty Smokers, free again,
The designated smoke-break has begun.
You guard your cigarettes against the rain
And puff blue clouds that half-obscure the sun.
You must stand fifteen feet away
From your home base's portico,
Your fingers blue, your faces grey,
You concentrate on that tip's cheery glow.

Oh silent outlaws from high offices
Filled with a plastic disinfectant smell
I tell you, once upon a tumour
I struggled up and out of Dirty Smoker Hell.

So here I stand, the re-born, pristine one
Who misses all the Dirty Smoker fun.

"WOULD YOU MIND! I'M TRYING TO SMOKE!!"

LIVE IT LIKE YOUR LAST DAY

Dig what can be dug

In the tunnel from Kennedy
the ceiling of metal or plastic
or plasticised metal or metalled plastic
reflects the red tail lights
of a hundred moving automobiles

like a river of red light
I told my Albanian cabdriver
who never noticed it before

I said that's my job
noticing stuff like that –
I'm a poet

An upside down
river of red light,
he said laughing.

Now you're doing it,
I said.

AT THE DELI

At Barney Greengrass The Sturgeon King
I had a rendezvous with Paula Harrington
my lovely student from Wesleyan
we hadn't met for thirty years

She wore a bright red mail-order catalogue coat
and she had cut short her long dark 60s hair
and her face shone and her dark eyes
were just as bright as thirty years ago
just as bright and deeper even maybe

And we sat there a couple of hours in the palace
of Barney Greengrass The Sturgeon King
and the sturgeon slices were delicious
but not as much as my reunion
with my lovely student from Wesleyan
As we talked together for thirty years
and we walked twenty blocks
and before we parted at 108th
we decided there shall be no more killing
because killing only leads to more killing
and this might take 300,000 years
or thirty days
but we decided that all the killing must stop
me and my lovely student
who is now a beautiful professor

THE REALLY GOOD OLD DAYS.
or The Underbelly of HISTORY

THE BOY-STY *(from the Unholy Bible)*

God didn't have to say: Let there be Singing –
It was always around.
Small tufty clouds of wordsong
Sailing bravely through the skies of Chaos.
Fish bubbling their favourite notes
Even as they found stumpy legs
Were beginning to grow from their undercarriages.
As soon as they smelled the air
All the animals burst into a thousand songs
And the trees and the rivers
Sang in green and sang in silver
And each of the stones had its own
Strong and silent song.

Each evening the yawning sun
Sang a fresh lullaby
And the choir of stars.
So much larger and brighter then,
So close they tickled the back of your neck,
Chanted their anthems to Adam and Eve
Who thanked them with human being singing.

When Adam and Eve named the Animals and Birds
that was the first great Song.
But after the Serpent and the Tree
and the Apple and the Fall and all,
After Adam and Eve were chased out of the Garden
By the Secret Police with Wings,
They moved to a muddy and stony little farm
East of Eden, in the hills of Groan,
Where singing was prohibited.

The ground was rough and rocky and relentless.
As soon as Cain and Abel could walk
The boys were put to work.
Cain dug the garden and grew Brussels sprouts,
Carrots, curly kale and spuds.
Abel looked after the sheep and pigs
Very kindly till it was time to eat them.
But however hard the family worked
They could never afford foreign holidays
And certainly had no spare time
For singing the forbidden songs of Eden.
Oh, a busy family is a grumpy family.

ADAM
It's not fair, nothing's fair.
We're being punished horribly by God.

EVE
It's not so bad for Cain and Abel,
They never knew Eden
So they don't miss it.

ADAM
What those boys need is a bit of punishing.
All they do is dig holes in the ground
Or watch flocks by night.
Mostly they slouch around humming to themselves,
Free as pterodactyls and about as useful.

EVE
We could make a kind of pig-sty for them
And keep them in there.

ADAM
A sort of big Boy-Sty – yes –
With a little stone hut
And they'd have to stay in the hut
And sit still and pay attention
And not hum for hours at a time.

EVE
Well, we could let them out on a patch of grass
Now and then for a stoneball match.
Just for a break.

ADAM
They'd run away.

EVE
No, the patch would have a stone wall round it,
Like the pigs have.

ADAM
What would they do all day in the Boy-Sty?

EVE
We could teach them about the Garden
And about our Punishment.
And then they would be sad like us.

All this was done, and Cain and Abel
Were taken every morning to the Boy-Sty.
And there they sat in a straight line
And were told about the Garden
And the Punishment and No Singing.

But one day God was driving by
And ordered his chauffeur to stop.
He called Adam and Eve to him
And demanded they explain the Boy-Sty.
When they had done so, God almost smiled at them.
He told them that they had founded the First School
And congratulated them and said
That perhaps they were beginning to learn the First Lesson –
About being Miserable Sinners.
But their Boy-Sty would not be a Real School
Without an External Examiner.

God said he would return each week
And examine Cain and Abel.
This is the first examination stone which God set:

Tablet One: Poetry.
1. Chip out the Supreme Poem.
(Answer: I AM THAT I AM).
2. Chip out the Human Being Poem.
(Answer: I AM A MISERABLE SINNER).

Tablet Two: Natural History.
1. How do you kill a sheep?
2. How do you kill a pig?

Cain put up his hand and asked
If there wasn't a tablet about Gardening.
God told him not to be stupid
And smote Cain's hand with boils.
Eve handed out stone tablets,
Hammers and chisels to the class.
God looked at the gold sun-watch on his wrist.
Start chipping – NOW! said God.

Cain and Abel both engraved their first tablets
In twenty-four hours.
But at the end of the exam
Cain handed in a wretched Tablet Two.
I don't know nowt about animals, he said.
I've written a song about grass instead.

God sent him to the bottom of the Class
And smote his arse with boils.

Next day, when Abel woke up,
Cain was nowhere to be seen.
Abel had a quick breakfast of raw lamb,
Then he strolled down to the Boy-Sty School,
Whistling under his breath.
Cain was crouching in the shadows of the Boy-Sty.
He held his hammer in his left hand,
His chisel in his right.

The Plays What I Wrote by Shakespeare

My name's William Shakespeare
  best poet in Britain
  these are the plays
  what I have written

I've mainly tried to use this system –
In the order I wrote them down to list 'em
With rhymes to help you learn their monickers –
One of the first was *Titus Andronicus*.
(That was full of wild and gory terrors).
I nicks *The Comedy of the Errors*
From a Plautus play about mixed-up twins;
The audience likes it so I begins
A piece about lovers double-crossed
Pessimistically named *Love's Labours Lost*.
A historical chronicle next I picksth
The *First*, *Second* and *Third* parts of *Henry the Sixth*.
I use all the wickedest tales I've heard
To celebrate villainous *Richard the Third*.
Then I have a hit with *The Taming of the Shrew*
About men and women and the nonsense they do.

Most people remember *Two Gentlemen of Verona*
For Crab the dog and Launce his owner.
My history of England rolls on and on
With one of my least popular plays – *King John*.
But I quickly recover with my biggest hit yet –
Ever-loving *Romeo and Juliet*.
Time for more Histories, my Director reckoned
So I nippily scribbles down *Richard the Second*
But tops it with *Henry Four Parts One and Two*
Which introduces Falstaff and his Krazy Krew.
Then lovers and fairies form the magical theme
Of my favourite *A Midsummer Night's Dream*.

A flashback tale, *The Merry Wives of Windsor*,
Brings good old Falstaff back agin, sir.
Then the uncomfortable *Merchant of Venice*
With Christian justice versus Jewish menace.
War make it feel great to be alive
Is my main message in *Henry the Five*.
Next comical sex-war sets the groundlings buzzing –
Beatrix and Benedick – *Much Ado About Nuzzing*.

Each new play is staged – they wouldn't dare spike it
After my hit comedy – *As You Like It*.
And I makes another romantic kill
With *Twelfth Night or What You Will*.
Then I tackle that famous geezer
London's favourite Roman *Julius Caesar*.
For good luck I wear a magical amulet
While I'm writing my masterpiece *Hamulet*.

Love will find a way, in a nutshell,
That's your *All's Well That Ends Well*.
Most of my lovers have ended up blesseder
Than the ill-fated *Troilus and Cressida*.
There's ethical mayhem and illegal pleasure
In the moral maze of my *Measure for Measure*.
A human fiend, Iago, torments a fellow
Of simple nobility named *Othello*.
But the greatest of my lines you'll hear
In the heart-shaking *Tragedy of King Lear*.
While insane ambition and sudden death
Rule the bleak Scotland of *Macbeth*.

Honest *Timon of Athens* comes to the belief
That every man is a born thief.
Mad, passionate love etcetera
Are practised by *Antony and Cleopetera*.
The People are two-faced as the god Janus –
But they are denounced by *Coriolanus*.
Less easy to understand than these
Is the rambling fairy tale of *Pericles*
And I'd just been given a vat of good wine
Before starting work on *Cymbeline*.

True love may suffer, but cannot fail
Is the mixed moral of *The Winter's Tale*.
My last play of all can't be called great
A mixed-up pageant – *Henry Eight*.
But I'll end by naming one of my best –
Magical-lyrical – *The Tempest*.

And if anyone asks who composed this ritual
it was done, without shame, by Adrian Mitual
    who loves William Shakespeare
        best poet in Britain
    and these are the plays
        what he has written.

About the Child Murderer Marie Farrar

by **BERTOLT BRECHT**

1

Marie Farrar, aged sixteen, born in April.
No birthmarks, bent by rickets, orphaned.
Apparently of good behaviour till
She killed a baby – this is how it happened.
She claims that, in the second month of pregnancy,
She went to a woman in a basement room
Who gave her two injections to abort it.
Which, she says, hurt – but the child stayed in the womb.
    But you, please don't be angry or upset.
    We all need all the help that we can get.

2

Well, anyway, she says, she paid.
She laced her corset very tight,
Drank schnapps with pepper, but that only made
Her vomit half the night.
Her belly was now visibly swollen.
When she washed up, she was in agony.
She was, she says, a young girl and still growing.
She prayed to Mary, very hopefully.
    And you, please don't be angry or upset.
    We all need all the help that we can get.

3

Her prayers turned out to be, it seems, useless.
It was a lot to ask. She put on weight.
At early mass her head was full of dizziness.
She knelt at the altar covered in cold sweat.
But still she kept her condition secret
Till, later on, birth took her by surprise.
She was so unattractive that
Nobody thought temptation could arise.
    And you, please don't be angry or upset.
    We all need all the help that we can get.

4

On the day itself, she says, just about dawn
She was scrubbing the stairs, when suddenly
Great nails clawed at her guts. She is torn.
But still, she keeps the secret of her pregnancy.

All day long, as she's hanging out the washing,
She thinks and thinks – then all at once she knows
She should be delivered. Her heart is heavy.
She finishes work late. Then up the stairs she goes.
    But you, please don't be angry or upset.
    We all need all the help that we can get.

5

As she lay down, they called her downstairs. Right away.
She must sweep up the newly-fallen snow.
That took until eleven. It was a long day.
She had no time to give birth till night. And so
She brought forth, so she says, a son.
This son was like all others that are born.
But she was not like other mothers – though
I find that I can't think of her with scorn.
    And you, please don't be angry or upset.
    We all need all the help that we can get.

6

So now I'd like to go on telling
The story of what happened to this son,
(She wants, she says, not to hide anything),
So what I am and what you are is clear to everyone.
She'd just climbed into bed, when she felt sick.
She was all alone. She wanted to shout.
She didn't know what was going to happen
But managed to stop herself crying out.
    And you, please don't be angry or upset.
    We all need all the help that we can get.

7

Her room was cold as ice, so she,
With her last strength, crawled to the lavatory
And there, she doesn't know when exactly,
Gave birth to a son without ceremony
Just before morning. She was, she says,
All muddled up, she did not know
If her freezing hands could hold on to the child
Because the servants' toilet was adrift with snow.
    And you, please don't feel angry or upset.
    We all need all the help that we can get.

8

Between her room and the lavatory.
(Nothing happened till this point, she insists),
The child started crying unbearably, so she
Beat it, blindly, without stopping, with both fists,
And went on beating it till it was quiet, she says.
And then she took it into bed
And kept it with her all through the night
And hid it, the next morning, in a shed.
    But you, please don't be angry or upset.
    We all need all the help that we can get.

9

Marie Farrar, aged sixteen, born in April,
Died in the Meissen jail.
This guilty single mother will
Show that all creatures of the earth are frail.
You who give birth in clean and comfortable beds
And call your pregnancy a blessed state,
Do not condemn the wretched and the weak –
Their sins are heavy, but their suffering is great.
    And so, please don't be angry or upset.
    We all need all the help that we can get.

version by Adrian Mitchell
literal translation by Karen Leeder

UNHISTORICAL ANTI-DOCUMENTARY

My plays are about
the day after tomorrow –
not about today

GRENDEL'S GROOVE

GRENDEL'S GROOVE

(for Gordon and Maeve)

The Beowulf saga told from the point of view of the Monsters

This Saga has the Grand Brand of Approval of the Universal Monster Club

The Universal Monster Club was founded in 1954 for the study and encouragement of Monsters in literature and life. The dictionary definition of a Monster accepted by the UMC is: 'A creature to be wondered at; a marvellous beast.' This would exclude mentally and physically deformed human beings, but would include the Unicorn and Grendel.

UMC members often watch movies like *The Creature from the Black Lagoon* or *King Kong* or *The Mole People* to cheer the monsters and heckle the bad human actors. In a typical monster films the Beast is sleeping peaceably at the bottom of the ocean in a gigantic ice cube when some mad scientists decide to test a nuclear bomb on him. This activates the Beast, which, understandably vexed, heads for the skyscraper areas of New York or Tokyo or Sheffield and proceeds to berserk.

In a similar plot-line, the Geats in the story of *Beowulf* decide to build an extremely noisy gastro-pub smack bang in the middle of Grendel's ancestral swamp – to their cost.

Those who would prefer the Official Line on the *Beowulf Saga* should note that there are marvellous and faithful versions of the original by three fine poets – Edwin Morgan, Seamus Heaney and Kevin Crossley-Holland. Shame they all chose the wrong side.

The voices you are about to hear in *Grendel's Groove* are:
GRENDEL
WENDEL, Grendel's mother
SYCORAX, a witch
WULFBANE, a double-headed dragon

WENDEL
>Biding our time,
>deep down here,
>biding our squelchy time...

>Been long time
>down in the Mere,
>long biding waterlogged time...

In our world of waving weaving weeds
curling currents among greeny groves,
>before people and porpoises,
>before leopards and lizards,
in the days of the dragons and dinosaurs,
>we was here,
>when ocean was a puddle.

My Dada was Cain the Killer.
Old Good God burned a brand on his face,
made him to live out in the wildness,
as the Bad God of War and Hell.

Only monsters would mate with Dada
but he have many matings
and make wonderful weirdful children.

One day dada Cain the Killer
found this beautiful gloopy mere,
one of Hell's holiday resorts,
and fell in love with its dread deeps,
>its murky soulsoup,
>its darling darkling depths,
>its benighted shadowcreatures,
>its softly silences.

Me, Wendel, was the child of his loving
with a swampthing something,
a marshmonster so oozily amorous
that I was born pregnant
with my only son and song –
I calls him Grendel.

Cain the Killer go off round the world
to do more murder and monster-loving.
Cain was bad company anyway –
only talked to his invisible brother.

Wendel and Grendel
we settle down in the mere's mudbottom
beside a silver underwater spring.

We feed each other from waterweed garden
and mudfish farm
and sing together
songs like
glooper bloop glooper blop

But after one, two, many, er, too many centuries
I hear a bang bang bang upstairs
on the ceiling of our swamp.
I calls out to my boy:

'Groodle, Grundle, Gramble Grendel!
Wake youself up, little Grimbel!
There's a terrible thunderhoofing on the roofing,
Sound like a forest marching in bangboots,
keeping old Wendel awake,
tangling and jangling her poor brainbox.
Grendel go up and tell them
cool it or else or else.'

GRENDEL
And so, from way deep down
and up out of the mulch and the munchy muckstuff
swim the mightiest me –
Grendel, full of the power of the pond.

I arise out of the munchy muckstuff
to the moonblessed surface.
Alone I walk the werewolf way
beside our murky, quakey Mere.

Then I see the place of people –
one, two, many, er, too many new trees in the ground,
no branches from their breasts,
bare of all bark, no tufts on tops,
stand all like an oblong orchard.
Grendel grasp one new tree out of its hole
and lift it above my mudhead.
No roots, O these new trees have no roots at all.

But inside the woody oblong,
rising up and screaming metalspeak at me
many too many of those fairy tale creatures –

people all feeding their fat faces.
I know they must be the Geats of Scandia.

I Grendel rumble and lumber
into this feasting forest of fools,
looking so feeble and feckless –
howsumever, with good cheer I greets the Geats:

'Hey you shrimps with painted shells,
sardines in clanging scales of metal –
Grendel greet you.
Friend Grendel bring you
great gouts of gruel by the clawful,
soul soup of the swamp!'

To refuse the gift of a monster guest
is to show insane insolence.
But these Geat skinnies are insulting,
swearing as they swarm,
bizzing and buzzing around me.
Picking and pricking me
with their silver stings.

'Aarogh!,' I quoth,
'Poke me not with limpy lances
or twang those sparrow snaparrows
or smack at me with swords
wrought badly from blubber –
these may tickle Grendel
but beware of my great Giggling.
Throw no goblets Grendelwards
nor pelt me sirrahs with silly plates
or the Glee of Grendel
may be the last laugh you –
Oi, I warned you!'

Ho ho I eat the first headfirst.
Ho ho I eat the second feetfirst.
Ho ho I drink the blood of the third
to salt and sweeten my mirthful thirst.
Ho ho I crunches the fourth like a bird.
Ho ho the fifth go down like a cherry.
The sixth and seventh men I do munch
Are so boozefull I get even more merry
As I swallow three more to complete my lunch.
So there's no one left in the empty seats
To ask why Grendel laughs while he eats.

Now the treetomb room is deadly quiet.
I skates across the deep carpet of blood
and down through the floor to Mama Wendel.

We get a few nights of deep peace
down in the swamp –
Then more bangs and yowlings
and warrior monkeytricks
and squeaky screams.
Those bald bodies, those pinkrat people
honk in their hall and snore like sawyers.
They breach the peace of my motherland Mere,
that deep broth where I was given birth,
hairy as a heath or a matted mammoth.

'All right, Mama!' –
Up I swims again
and goes through the menu
and brings back a dozen
assorted Geats for Mama
still warm and spouting
their red gravy.
We have a full and funny meal
Loads of laughs.

Next night – whambangle hammerheads
Sounds worse than ever.
These squeaky sardines never learn –
I go up to teach em.

As I go in
they all fade away
out into the midnight dim starlight.
But one big people
strides on to the floor.
No armour
no clothes
no weapons.
I am Beerywulf, he bellows,
And his voice be huge and shining.

Beerywulf and Grendel,
big and bigger.
We crouch,
move at angles.
We collide –
the house of his flesh
against my swamp-castle.

My claws clever,
his hands huge and heavy.
I laugh and bite lump from
this foolish stranger.
then he takes my right claw
in both his fists
and twists and turns.
My arm resists
but its sinews rip
from wrist to shoulder
he twists and turns
and my whole arm burns
and is wrenched raggedly
off at my shoulder.

Now I do not laugh
for I know death is in the doorway.
My black-bleeding arm
drops to the floor.
Beerywulf advances.
I run and dive
out of that corpse-orchard
down into the beautiful
dark depths of the swamp.

There Mama Wendel nurses me
with all the magic medicines
which sprout deep in the quagmud.

    WENDEL
I am an angry doctor to my son.
I put him under a spell of sleeping.
Secretly I rise to the surface to spy on the Geats.
Woodbutchers and colour-splashers
work to repair the place
wrecked by Grendel's brave battling.

I watch Beerywulf being rewarded
for ridding the place of Grendel, my son.
I watch them give him gold
and horses and armour
as they celebrate that bare brute with songs and poems
and a great banquet.
After their feasting
now they lay them down to sleep.

I pad silently
into the hall of drunken dreamers.
I stand stone-struck
There is his poor
arm and claw
nailed to the wooden wall.

I need my Grendel's arm.
Grendel must be mended.
I prise off the prize
Then a shout goes up
from some Geat git:

'Uh oh –
here comes Grendel's *Mother*,
and she's three times his size!'

I run and dive back down
to boghome mosshospital.
I begins a slow and gentle operation
embroidering back my son's gashed arm,
singing the spells
to heal his harm,
in deepwater nursery
where he was born.

But waterworld is suddenly invaded –
down through the blue-black layers of coolness,
following Hrunting his magic sword,
dives that Beerywulf slaughterman.

As he swims down past mosshospital window
I grabs him good,
swoops him up in my branches
and carries him down into
the deeps of Waterhell.
He swing his magic Hrunting at me
but: 'You can't cut me
like you can't cut water!'
Ho ho I say –
I getting hungry.

Underwater wrestling now.
He throw me on to the mudbed.
Me bounce up and throw him back
but just as I go to finish him
the coward calls on God.

God shines a light on
my old battleaxe
left me by the good old giants.
Beerywulf grab it, swirl it
smash it in my neck
and there goes my head,
floating past me.

And Beerywulf kick my head like a football
then rises back into the upper air
to become one great big hairy Hero.

Now it's desperate hard work in mosspital.
I'm still sewing on Grendel's arm
but without being able to see
because of being headless.
Meanwhile Grendel tries to balance
my head on my neck
and sew it back
all with one claw.

By the time we finish,
it's party time again upstairs.
we decide it's time to ask for help.
We call in Sycorax the water-witchard.
She is a monster life-coach and she says:

    SYCORAX
Get out of the Mere.
Swamps are over.
It'll be drained before you're three hundred.

Look, she says, Cain and I were like that –
So I owe you something.
There's a daft king just died.
He's buried way out in the wilderness
down a secret tunnel in a cave
under a mountain without a name.
He lost his kingdom and his subjects,
all his warriors and his mind as well –
but even as a skellington
he hangs on to his treasure.
Ingots diamond tiaras
mixed glittergem crown sets
emeralds marbles,
one heap of blinding bling.

Now loot like that needs security
so here's my plan.
You two get on well, I know.
Why not sew yourselves,
Mother and Son,
on to and into each other?
Then I'll turn you into one
two-headed fire-breathing Dragon.
You can guard the daft king's treasure
for ever and ever.
Just wrap your scaliness all around it.
If any smartarse tries to nick it –
one double blast of dragon-breath –
they're toast!

Now you have sewn yourselves together
I give you your new name.
You are now the Dragon Wulfbane.
Go now, you'll not see Sycorax again
until the day you die your doubledeath.

   WULFBANE
Then we flies off on our new dragonflick-wings
over to the mountain in the wilderness
into the treasure cave.
We curls ourselves round the gleaming jewels
keeping warm with our own red hot breathing
and settling down to the first beautiful snooze
of the peaceable double dragon Wulfbane.
Wulfbane dreaming his dragon dreams.

Fifty years later –
waking up, shaking up,
feeling dry –
we hears a clatter in the secret tunnel.
Some runaway slave
must have fell in –
he crawls along,
hand touches golden goblet,
hears double snorings of Wulfbane –
yells and scoots,
still clutching goblet.
As he vanishes we sees him
by the light of the flames of our breath
we sees his back as he vamooses
whip stripes all over his back.

Slave on the run
with nothing but a golden goblet –
of course he gets caught and hooded
and put through the questions
and suddenly our treasure hoard
is page one news!

We go out for a flight one day,
gliding around, seeing the sights.
Get back and see
a whole trainload of shining stones
chuffing and puffing away
from our stone home
taking our treasure
to the city of the Geats.

Wulfbane Doubledragon
doubleangry.
Wait for midnight to take off –
circle the moon three times
then dive on Geatsville.
Lick over all its houses seven times
with our flame-thrower tongues
then lash them into ruins
with the whambam whips
of our mighteous tails.
That's good that's right –
that's Doubledragon fun.

Good long sleep after that
but when we wake up,
look out to double-snuff the dew,
what do we sniff but the bodysweat
of that slave gobletsnatcher
and there he is,
and alongside him a parade of Geats
playing hero horns
and bearing on their shoulders
the burly burden of
the seventy year old superhero –
Beerywulf the Bloody.

And he shout out blunderwords
doing his big boast thing,
but his voice quivers and quavers
as Beerywolf wearywolf tries to bellow:
come out you dragon devil!
let me skin you for ladies' handbags!

That prehistoric hero got head full of muscle.
Doubledragon got doublebrain.
Wulfbane lie doggo and connive and connive.
We not blink, we say nowt,
we know he's coming in.

There go his clumpsteps –
we give him double hotbreath,
we give him double thunder,
we give him little taste
of hellfire.

But on he come
into the dark treasure hall.
By the light of our flames
and the light of our jewels
we see the wrinkling bullyboy

So we swing ourself round
and we snake him around
and we burn up his ground
till he dance to the sound
of our roar in the mound.

Then he slash out his sword
but it move in slomo,
slips off our scales
and we laugh our ho ho
we is Wulfbane!
and see his eyes jump in their sockets
as he sees both our heads
as he realise
he face the Grendel Wendel doubledragon
and he turn away.
End of round one.
Takes two to tangle –
Beery come back with a boy wonder
Wiglaff the Shelfing
or Frogliff the Shellfish.
But our first bad breath
turn little Wiggle's shield
into black ashes.

Then the old junkpile Beery
swing his sword at our skulls,
but it bounce and break.
End of round two.

So Wulfbane charge again.
We flood him with flame.
Sensing a Beerywulf barbecue,
we dig two double sets of razor-fangs
into his withery leather neck
so that it spurt red! red! red!
a life-death fountain.

But Figleaf the Elfling,
his titchy sidekick,
does dip and slip under our bellies
and stick upwards, once, twice.
Wulfbane falter and fail,
heartflames sputtering.

Then blood-spouting Beerywulf pull his dagger
and staggers up to stick it stuck
between our dragonribs.

Suddenly we see Sycorax
she look so beautiful
we know we dying.
Grendel and Wendel
and the doubledragon
Wolfbane
all dying together.

Our four great eyes mist over.
We see our enemy's neckwound
bulging with dragonvenom
surging into his bloodstream,
down towards his heart.

We tell Sycorax:
it was exciting
it was fun
but kind of useless.

Grendel and Wendel
could have been with Sycorax
all together sitting round
in our waterweed garden
beside the silver underwater spring,
drinking swampjuice,
swapping mad and marvellous stories
with Beerywolf and Wigless the Sizzling

and singing together
songs like
glooper bloop glooper blop.

But seems it had to be
murder for murder –
the end of Beerywulf
the end of us.

goodbye Grendel
goodbye Wendel
goodbye Sycorax
goodbye everybody

glooper bloop glooper blop

ACADEMIC FOOTNOTES TO GRENDEL'S GROOVE

GEATS: they came from southern Sweden and built their Hall on the island of
Zealand which would become, many centuries later, handy for Copenhagen.

WULFBANE: the dragon in *Grendel's Groove*, unlike the dragon in *Beowulf*,
has a name (and also a miraculous conception). I chose Wulfbane in honour
of the talking picture *The Wolfman* (with Lon Chaney), in which the following
chilling quatrain is recited by sinister central European peasants several
times:

> *Even a man whose heart is pure*
> *And says his prayers at night*
> *May turn into a Wolf when the Wolfbane blooms*
> *And the autumn moon is bright.*

ENJOY THE LIGHT

GREAT LIVES

RALPH STEADMAN 2°08

LOVE, FRIENDSHIP and SHEEP

In my dream, all the wisest people in the world had come together at an observatory on a hill to decide if the stars were trying to communicate with us, or whether they were meaningless. After some years of trying to decode celestial movements, they were about to give up when some excited children pulled them outside and pointed up to the night sky, where the stars were spelling out, in enormous shining star-letters, the words:

 ENJOY THE LIGHT.

I woke up with those words branded on my memory. It seemed like very good advice and I have tried to follow it.

DEATH IS SMALLER THAN I THOUGHT

My Mother and Father died some years ago
I loved them very much.
When they died my love for them
Did not vanish or fade away.
It stayed just about the same,
Only a sadder colour.
And I can feel their love for me,
Same as it ever was.

Nowadays, in good times or bad,
I sometimes ask my Mother and Father
To walk beside me or to sit with me
So we can talk together
Or be silent.

They always come to me.
I talk to them and listen to them
And think I hear them talk to me.
It's very simple –
Nothing to do with spiritualism
Or religion or mumbo jumbo.

It is imaginary.
It is real.
It is love.

Our Mother

blue eyes, silver hair...
so close, all we see is a
lovely blur of her

her eyes were
April the 24th blue
as she weeded the borders
she knelt on the moss

Our Father

his face was gracefully
carved from oak
you heard Scotland
when he spoke

his silence was
deep as a well
he had served four years
in the trenches of Hell

EARLY DAZE.

I was born on the Moon
On a sunlit night
it was Saint Diablo's Day
My Egg cracked apart
with a happy heart
I dived into the Milky Way

I was found in that bath
by my Father and Mother
A Unicorn and a Dove
They took me to their home
In an ice-cream Dome
And all they ever taught me was to do with Love
And everything they taught me was to do with Love

44 %

73

KAY ON THE PICCADILLY LINE

on a London Underworld train
overcrowded with shadows
she shines
with a calm and comforting light
the lady standing by the doors
with the soft white hair

she is in charge
of a mixed grill of young men and women
with the smiles and puzzlement and tantrums
of grown-up children
who would not get very good marks
for talking or for thinking

Warren Street! says the tannoy
and a wrapped-up girl repeats
Warren Street, Warren Street, Warren Street –
reassuring herself

I want to rest my feet
snarls the unsmiling handsome lad
the small Oriental boy
laughs to himself because
so much is funny
and the wrapped-up girl
in the big blue hat
overflows with joy

the white-haired lady calms them
only two stops to go
then we'll be off
I want to be off, says a happy one

the unsmiling lad scrambles and bags a seat
snarling at least I've got a seat at last

everyone's excited when they reach South Kensington
I hope they're going to the stuffed animal museum

the lady gathers them together
she wears her white hair like a sail
they follow in her wake
I'm sorry to see them go

her touch is so light and affectionate
I want to say to the lady
they're very lucky to have you
but I know she will reply
I'm very lucky to have them
How do I know?

because she is just like my mother
just like Kay

on the platform at Earls Court
they have a metal bench set in the concrete
where you can sit and cry for your mother
that's where I sat

2 April 2008

ON THE PICCADILLY LINE AGAIN

One of the man's trembling hands
fluttered around his head
like a lost white bird

he was excited but it was hard to speak
but he leaned forward and
HOME he said HOME
HOME.

I said: you're going home?
that's good

HOME he said
HOME – MUM
and suddenly both his hands
performed a knife and fork dance
in front of his smiling mouth

Mum will make you a good meal?
MM HOME – MUM
and he gave himself a loving hug

we shook hands a few times
in celebration
of his homecoming meal

he showed me his travel pass
and I helped him fit the ticket in it

we shook hands again
HOME he said
and looked at the other passengers
and mostly they responded
with a thumbs up

and all the time the cheerful woman opposite
responded to everything with a smile
and a touch
and prepared him to move him into his wheelchair

HOME – MUM
and most of the carriage waved Goodbye

SOME MEANINGS OF THE WORD JILLPIRRIE.

(for that fine poet and teacher, Jill Pirrie)

a. a silver mountain stream's memories of the ocean.
b. a tall knitted hat with brightly-coloured spirals worn
       by dancing cooks, animal fools and Tibetan balloonists.
c. snow out of a clear blue sky.

BEATTIE AS SMIKE

(at Gospel Oak School on 14 July 1978,
her last performance in her last term)

small   determined
she pushes an invisible heavy trunk
   all the way across the floor
 has to bend her backbone right down
to get her shoulders square behind the trunk
   and gather her body for the long heave
she pushes two more invisible heavy trunks
   all the way across the floor

those trunks are in the wrong place stupid
            push them all back

down on all fours she concentrates
      her weight and her muscles
            into her hands
then she gathers her body for the long shove
      one by one pushes all three
heavy invisible trunks back into place.

there's a lazy character annoying her
she pushes an invisible trunk in his way
      he trips   heavily   over it

Beattie/Smike walks to the front of the stage
      the long curtains close behind her
            she takes her stand
      she holds her right forearm
            with her left hand
      which is not a random gesture
      but shows how cold she feels
she focuses on the clock at the back of the hall
      behind the Noah's Ark audience
            and begins to sing

            her low notes are rocks
            her high notes are jewels
      her low notes are the eyes of goats
her high notes are the eyes of humming-birds
            strongly she stands there
      and strongly her voice walks among us
                  blessing us

she stands so strong in love
parents, teachers, her sister and friends
        giving her strength

and suddenly singing behind her singing,
        the choir state most clearly
            that they love her

                so strong
            so strong in love
                so strong

(and when everybody cheers
she breaks out of character
            and smiles)

FRIENDS AND APPLES

(for Doug, Dawn and Devon Hall at Christmas)

these days I spend more time
   thinking of orchards

apple trees, grown beautiful with age,
   stretch their brown bodies and brown arms
      and sing the seasons:
         goldenfall
          barebones
            greenbuttons
          blossomstorm
            appletime

and the long green hair of orchards
impossible for mowing machines
so kind to lovers and children and fugitives

and the bumpy, home-made stone walls of orchards
      promising such secrets
      promising such treasure

     and the work of orchards
     so subtle and gradual
       the work of orchards –

    three apples
        in a bowl

   dark green midnight
    in the orchard

    the smile of the moon
     and the stars like freckles

      three apples fall without a sound
      from green down into green

        they are found in their nest
          of knee-deep grass

     three apples glowing
      in a green bowl

it was a long way for you to travel
all the way from old New Mexico
to gladden our little orchard

friends and apples
friends and apples

three apples
in a bowl
you are with us
in our house

you brighten our home
and you warm my soul

three apples
in a bowl

DOUG

(for Douglas Kent Hall, Dawn and Devon, with much love)

   good friend,
  sweet man of peace
seems you died so quietly
   so courteously

simply lay down
and waited for
whatever it is

you played the fool
looked after people
comforted and cheered
your friends and family
recorded the lives
of those around you
honouring them

   I never heard
a complaint from you
but at the smell of bullshit
   you'd harumph
with heart-shaking laughter

   oh dog-like Doug
   like Swansea Jack
that brave black Newfoundland
which rescued so many people
      from the sea

(you would be happy
to be talked of as a dog
you knew the souls of dogs
and many other animals)

scribbling this down
in the London Underground
I look at the people
packed into this carriage
fresh and faded
every race on earth
you would have understood
each one's special beauty

too sad to write
Doug, I simply send to you
    and those you love
my love for all your friendship
your voice deep as a cool well
        your bear-hug
your earthquake laughter
your quiet, wonder-working art
and your sweet courtesy.

2 April 2008

Seamus Heaney is never seen
Bouncing on a trampoline.
But on the flying trapeze –
He's the bee's knees.

EDWARD LEAR'S IMAGINATION
AS A
HELL TO HEAVEN MACHINE

Oh you shove your sadness down the Funnel
Push your terror through the Grinder
Take all those years of ugly tears
And fling them in the Binder

There'll be thrashing and smashing
Crashing and bashing
And ferocious jets of steam
But then the great Engine
Will stop its avenging
And melt into a melodious dream

As out steps the Pobble who has no Toes.
The courageous Jumblie Crew
And the Dong, the Dong with the Luminous Nose
And the Owl and the Pussycat too
    Bless you Mr Lear
And the Owl and the Pussycat too –

A VISIT TO IVOR

(for Ivor Cutler and all who loved him)

The seventh floor of the Royal Free.
In the television room
the screen was blank and silent.
Ivor sat facing two of his favourite friends –
Maggie and Joyce –
both of them sweet and strong
with the sort of smiles
make a man feel like living.

Ivor's eyes seemed empty
as he turned his face to me.
But the more I talked
the more I knew he remembered me.
I saw that sparkle.

He flipped over the bright pages
of the Jack B. Yeats catalogue I'd brought him
and smiled at the little illuminated Blake book.

Ivor said: What are you doing?
I said: Writing for children mostly.
do you remember when we did a TV show
and you brought some kids with you, Ivor?
You marched them round the studio
shouting their poems
and told them:
Speak up or I'll bite your heads off.
Ivor said: I don't remember biting their heads off.

I said I was sorry
I never took up his offer
of teaching me how to play blues piano.
Ivor said: It's not too late,
you can play.

He raised his left hand and brought it down on his left knee
gently over and over.
Then he introduced his right hand
playing his right thigh in another rhythm,
and all the time, over the two silent beats,
Ivor was talking about playing the piano,
how the two hands walk together but differently.

Then, with a strong gesture of his right hand,
he marked a line down the middle of his brow
all the way down to his thighs, saying:
And this is where the humanity enters the music.

It was a beautiful speech,
softly and soulfully spoken
and we leaned forward to catch his words
but often they were interrupted
by shouting or a wild cry from a nearby ward.
Each time, Ivor, who was in love with silence,
flinched from the sharp noises
scratching his brain,
then recovered and regained his lovely speech
about the beauty of piano playing.

Joyce and Maggie said that on another visit
they danced with Ivor,
and would he like to dance?
Would you like me to dance for you? he asked.
We all said Yes like children.

Ivor stood up, walked to the far corner of the room.
Waited.
He was making an entrance.
He backed against the corner, then stepped forth.
He stood, head bowed,
being nothing but a Beckett puppet.
One hand was lifted halfway, then dropped.
The other lifted halfway, dropped.
He took two ancient steps,
but then, at the moment when I felt like sobbing, somehow,
a bounce entered his feet –
at the moment when I felt like sobbing –
and his hands were on his hips –
he was flouncing along, swaying along,
throwing wicked glances over his shoulder,
eyes sparkling like glitterballs.
The bleak Television Room
became a Galactic Music Hall
for Ivor the Entertainer.

He bowed his head to our
love and laughter and applause.
He asked us to stand up. We did so.
He moved towards the door.

On the way he paused to pat his two new books –
'Blake' he said, and 'Yeats'
as if he were patting two favourite dogs.
We said: Goodbye, Ivor.

Goodbye, Ivor.
We do love you.

July 2006

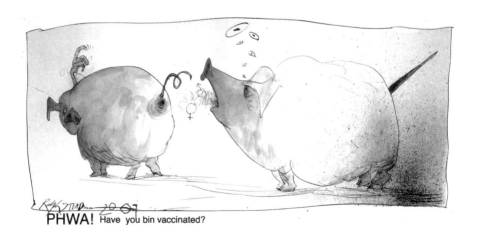

PHWA! Have you bin vaccinated?

To My Agent Nicki Stoddart

At ten in the morning I ring to say:
The Emperor of Jamnaphu
sent me a message on a golden scroll
saying: I want to start a theatre
and it shall be on a Mississippi showboat
which will sail around the Mediterranean
stopping at every welcoming port
all the year round
carrying a brilliant company
of actors, singers and musicians
utterly dedicated to the performing
of all your wonderful plays.

You gulp, but do not say:
Adrian you're daydreaming again,
there's no such Emperor.

You say mm, yes, all right.
I'll find out what I can about that.

By 10.30 P.M. I am snoring in bed
but you still sit
alone in the enormous office
surrounded by the 303 volumes of
Yellow Pages for South Eastern Asia
still trying to track down
The Emperor of Jamnaphu
for my sake.

Should he not exist –
you will create him.

HAPPY BIRTHDAY Ralph STEADman

You were born in walloping Wallasey,
In the middle of a stormy night
With your left hand on your willy
And a leaky pen in your right

'He's a gonzo Michaelangelo!'
Cried all of the nursing throng
So they handed you a ukelele
And everybody sang along –

Yes, they sang:
Hang on Steadman, Steadman hang on
Hang on Steadman, Steadman hang on

Ralph Steadman is a guy from a very dark part of the town
And snobby art fanciers sometimes try to put him down
Steadman just keep on doing what you got to do
And hang on Steadman, man, cos we all love you

that's why we sing:
Hang on Steadman, Steadman hang on
Hang on Steadman, Steadman hang on
Steadman just keep on doing what you got to do
And hang on Steadman, man, cos we all love you

Jackals from Surrey make billions out of arms supplies
And the snakes of war are hissing in the Parliament of Lies
But you're creating beauty which can celebrate or condemn
Working at the building of a city of love called the New Jerusalem

that's why we sing:
Hang on Steadman, Steadman hang on
Hang on Steadman, Steadman hang on

With Hunter S. Thompson you went on some heavy trips
A couple of icebergs floating round looking for ships
A thunderstorm broke and now your friend has gone
But hang on Steadman, man, keep on keeping on

and we'll sing:
Hang on Steadman, Steadman hang on
Hang on Steadman, Steadman hang on

You got Jehovah's number, you analysed Sigmund Freud
With drawings that left us freaked out and overjoyed
To Wonderland you danced in your black and white patent shoes
With Alice in your arms through the Looking-Glass and home to Loose

so we sing:
Hang on Steadman, Steadman hang on
Hang on Steadman, Steadman hang on

Anna's tapestries glow with her ever-loving fairytales
Sadie's making movies with magical children in Wales
May your friends all gather round you when you feel like a good sing-song
Just bring out your funky old banjo, and we'll all sing along

We'll sing:
Hang on Steadman, Steadman hang on
Hang on Steadman, Steadman hang on
Steadman just keep on doing what you got to do
And hang on Steadman, man, cos we all love you

WITH LOVE FOR MIKE WESTBROOK

on his 70th birthday

Performing my poems in a breezeblock arts centre Cape Town shanty town
I was shouting on the offbeat of the drummers next door and the red sun was
     diving down

Well an old guy sat on a wooden school desk and he had this killer guffaw
So I aimed my poems straight at him and he puffed and shouted for more

So I let him have a tonguetwister lyric with an old Chuck Berry beat
And he opened his mouth to show me three good teeth and he stomped with
     his blue suede feet

It was right at the height of the poem and I was pushing it I suppose
But my top set of false teeth popped out of my mouth and nearly bopped him
     on the nose

But I caught them just before they hit and I stuck them back in my gob
And I got a grip on the poem again and went on to finish the job

And of all the poetry gigs I've done that one is the brightest pearl
And Mike I dedicate it to you – for you are the Duke of Earl.

2 April 2006

92

you paint it
you pick up big brushes
you paint it

Disappointed OLD FART.
South AFRICA . 24.1.96
Ralph STEADman

MY GENIUS

My name is Linda.
I am a fourteen-year-old poet
in a huge class
in an enormous school
I don't know why

My desk is next to the desk
of Skruff, Boy Genius

Most of the kids
laugh at him
and call him Skruff
he looks through them

Teachers yell at him
Gangs try to pick on him
Come here, Skruff!!
he dodges them

But sometimes passes me
with a sideways smile
and it goes straight
to my heart

So I write poems for Skruff
not saying out loud
I love you
poems more like paper flowers

I give him poems
He gives me a smiles

I think maybe
Skruff hasn't got a home
I daydream about him
I've started to write
whole books about him

SKRUFF is the first book
and it introduces him
living in the woods with
his white dog Shadow

ROUGH SKRUFF is the second
and it tells how
he outwits a gang
called the Badnecks

SKRUFF LOST is about him
(and Shadow) going on a journey
to find his Mum and Dad

SPOTLIGHT ON SKRUFF
is about him getting to be
a famous pianist like Jools Holland
(this one's a bit fantastic)

SKRUFF GONE is the last one
that I've done
and is about Skruff disappearing
this is a sad one

I have written all five books
and illustrated them
all ready for his birthday
on April 24th

The SONG of the Cross of St. Protet

(for John and Astrid Furnival, with love)

the dove dives down
through a starry ring
to bless the mother
    hovering
as the cross shudders
then begins to fly
    on its journey
to the sky's blue eye

    the mother
lies in a deep dream
holding her hands
over the crossbeam
    so nobody
shall ever again
be nailed upon it
she takes all their pain

    Erik Satie's skull
    proffers two logs
baguettes or crossbones
    to favourite dogs

a dancing heart
  tiptoes alone
down a path which winds
  like a saxophone

there's a sketchbook of stone
    propped against the cross
    filled with gentle drawings
      of love and loss

    and here's the anvil rock
which heard young Arthur's laughter
when he drew from it so easily
    the cross they call Excalibur

DRAWING OPPOSITE BY JOHN FURNIVAL

97

SHEEPISHLY ~ ... ... ——

*(written in the week after the deaths of three of my friends –
Tilly Laycock, John La Rose and Ivor Cutler)*

between the fields of waking
and the fields of dreaming

so many of those old
  limestone walls
    have crumbled down

gaps in the walls

waking   walking
in the wake of the waves of my dreams
waking walking
in the dawn as it dawns upon me

I am no Tyger
I am no Lamb
At seventy-three
I am a senior sheep

high up on the dales by day
down flat in the swamps at night
daydreaming moondreaming
shadowdancing
in a Samuel Palmer countryside

but don't imagine
I'm not working bloody hard
for the New Jerusalem

I'm growing visionary sweater-wool
to keep the children warm
as I stand here
gaping at the gaps

visionary wool
which will be woven
into tapestries and coverlets
and scarves and mittens
of that great country-city of peace

my wool is often wild
multi-coloured and exciting
but sometimes softer
creamy and comforting

much of my work is done
by mountain waterfalls
head low munching heather
ears brushing the bracken
and a sniff of ice in the highland air

and some of my work is done
on the rich green banks
of casual muddy southern rivers

it's not all the same to me
but I'm all the same to them

these meadows I survive in
frosty or fiery
celandine or olive tree

I'm happy to meander
from one to the other
tasting so many different weathers
growing so many different dreams of wool

gaping at the gaps

This evening I'm watching that famous field
Anfield on the television
hoping that Liverpool will score
and Arsenal despair

from the Kop I trundle out
with my good dog to our dark garden
where I help her with my chanting
to squat and piddle

out of the garden
up the rocky stairs
towards the stone stars
and into bed
where a few wings of a book
fly me on to

a meadow of dreams
where any animal may enter
now the old limestone walls
have crumbled away

nowadays nowadays I meander
from dreamfield to wakefield
from amazement to grumpiness
from vision to radio
from stupidity to genius

but I keep on keeping on
I keep on keeping on
growing my wool
growing my wool of many colours

thank you

A WALK ON THE WEIRD SIDE

or BETTER OUT THAN IN

THIS MORNING'S DREAM

(21 June 2006)

I was prepared for a public lecture by being hypnotised in a dentist's chair by a man in a white coat whom I suddenly realised was Jools Holland.

I was very tense but suddenly went all loose. I opened my eyes to see Jools and a nurse with dark curly hair both laughing uproariously

'What's so funny?', I asked.

The nurse said: 'Well, we just moved all of the bad things out of your head and put in good things from mine.'

So here they are:

WONGO the WONDER DOG

(theme song for a new TV series)

Wongo the Wonder Dog
Smarter than the average cat
She can steal a bone
Eat a parking cone
And shit in your favourite hat
Wongo the Wonder Dog
Is definitely man's best friend
She can scramble an egg
While she's shagging your leg
She's the living end

Wongo the Wonder Dog
   Ah Wow!!

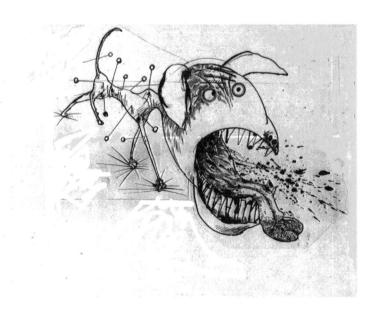

darling, we're ber-ake-ing up itseeems
could be your phone, maybibby mine
listen – I'll ring you in my dreams –
    ghosts on the line

make booze, not cars, the robots cry,
down the mass production belt pours blue wine
I'm too fucked-up to reason why –
    ghosts on the line

hang all your dirty laundry in a gallery
throw your clean clothes into the Serpentine
let plasticated corpses earn your salary –
    ghosts on the line

the London Underground regrets to say
this train's been stopped by a huge porcupine
who's singing *Yip-Eye-Addy-Eye-Ay-Eye-Ay* –
    ghosts on the line

the artist draws his love through tears
which drop and blotch that soft outline
he hasn't seen the woman for ten years –
    ghosts on the line

after I'm dead, I'll visit you each spring
as long as you consider you're still mine
later you may still hear me whispering –
    ghosts on the line

A LONG WALK

I was walking Daisy home and we started to cross the road. There was the whoosh of a car coming round the bend fast and a great white light. Then Daisy and I were over the road and walking home. The yellow of the morning sun had turned silvery. When we came to our house we walked straight through the front door into the hall. Celia and the cats paid no attention to us. I stroked the fur of Moonlight, but my hand felt nothing at all. Just then a transparent newspaper was pushed through a glass front-door panel. I picked it up off the mat. It was the Ghost Guardian. I took it with me to the kitchen where I found a package marked Ghost Dog Food. It was full of misty diamond biscuits. I poured some into a glass bowl for Daisy. Celia said to the cats: 'They're a long time today.'

CONFESSION: MY MACHINE

I keep on getting
good ideas
about how the world might work

they are often odd
usually unusual
face it they are sometimes barmy
but some of them seem to shine

best thing to do I think
about these good ideas
is to write them down
like I'm doing now

bits and pieces
not all connected up
bits and pieces
of the truth

they don't come into my mind
no they're not my ideas
if I tell you how I get them
will you keep it secret?
will you? promise?

they come in very small print
on yellowy paper
in torn off oblongs
which emerge
at irregular intervals
from a dark grey duct thing
sticking out of a sort of machine

the machine is a bit like
two black basins stuck together
face to face
stuck together permanently

the machine is very heavy
as if it were made mostly of lead
I found it one morning
in my front garden
and carried it in
to the kitchen table

looks a bit rough
said my daughter
and she was right

and it sat on the table
doing nothing
and I sat on a kitchen stool
watching it
do nothing

I wanted to inspect it closely
but I didn't have a magnifying glass
so I ran down the road
to the 99p shop
and they had three magnifying glasses
as a set for 99p

so I got them
brought them home
broke them out of their
transparent packaging

first thing I discovered
was a crack at the end of the duct thing
and protruding from the end of the duct thing
a piece of yellowy paper

so I pulled at the paper
which was soft to touch
and I tugged and it began
to emerge from the duct thing

and it said
do not worry too much about this
but read what I have to say
and think about it please

so I tore off the piece of paper
and held it in the palm of my hand
where it curled and then rocked
like a little cradle

and I whispered who are you?

then there was a small metallic growl
from deep inside the machine
and then a click

and out of the duct thing
pushed another piece of paper
which I tore off

and this one said:
don't worry about that
just read what I have to say
and if it's useful
use it

OK I said
and the next piece of paper said

have your breakfast
so I did

but then I had to go to work
so I told the machine I would be back
then put it in the cupboard under the sink
with the bleach and stuff

days and nights went past
and the only real bits of them seemed to happen
when I was sitting at the kitchen table
watching the machine

what is it, asked my daughter?
it's some sort of machine, I said.
Looks like it could've been a prehistoric laptop, she said.
Could've been, I said, could've been,
but I didn't know

I talked to it sometimes
but usually it ignored me
and just kept on producing
unproveable statements and
mysterious information
word pictures and lists
and numbers

I kept all the pieces of paper
in an old hatbox
they kept on coming

there is a mixture of red and green
which could soothe your pain

imagine the life of a sheep

and so on

at one point it looked at the rest of the year
and said
there will be two times this year
when a whole week goes soggy
and kind of sinks out of sight
one of these weeks
will probably be between
July and September
and the other, definitely, during Christmas

I thought the sayings of the machine
(I had begun to think of them as sayings)
must come from the mind
of a very wise or very mad prophet
given to mental drifting, visions and silliness
or from a class of mischievous children

But when I asked the machine
about its personality
it always changed the subject
which was easy
because it tended to jerk
from subject to subject
for no apparent reason
without apology

do cradles float? it asked

I began to think somebody might arrive to claim it
there was nothing in the papers
about a missing machine

three in the morning
the doorbell rang
the frontdoor crashed inwards
and the house was full of
armed police

they lined up everyone in the house
outside in the street
face down on the pavement
and handcuffed us

they found my machine
in the cupboard under the kitchen sink

we got you
we can keep you 28 days without a charge said the smallest cop
we'll need a sight longer than that, said the biggest cop
42 days and 42 nights would be more like it

BAN THE BANJO

I've got an instrument, I'd like to tell you
About the banjo plucking that I do
You can always hear me come
Cos I whistle and I hum
And I love to have a strum
Well wouldn't you?
I took me banjo into Church one Sunday
And stuck it on a cushion for a bit
But Parson knelt on it, then jumped in pulpit
And hollered down the aisle: 'Thou silly git!

That's a bloody silly place to put a banjo
You're a proper bloody fool to put it there
You can practise bloody daily
On your ukebloodylele
You can play Bill Bloody Bailey lad
And I don't care
You can hang your bloody banjo from the ceiling
You can stick it any other bloody where
But that's a bloody silly place to put a banjo
You're a proper bloody fool to put it there!'

Once I joined the local Philharmonia
Best in all the land without a doubt
I put me banjo case
In a most convenient place
Put a smile upon my face and sat about
Sir Malcolm Sargent mounted to the rostrum
And with each step the lusty cheers rang out
But he slipped on my banjo
And he fell on his – you know –
And the Corn Exchange re-echoed to the shout:

'That's a bloody silly place to put a banjo
You're a proper bloody fool to put it there
You can practice bloody daily
On your ukebloodylele
You can play Bill Bloody Bailey lad
And I don't care
You can hang your bloody banjo from the ceiling
You can stick it any other bloody where
But that's a bloody silly place to put a banjo
You're a proper bloody fool to put it there!'

Once I took a little trip to Blackpool
I was on me happy honeymoon
I stripped down to me vest
And said 'Would you like a rest?'
She said 'What I'd like the best
Would be a spoon.
She got into the bed, I climbed beside her
And snuggled with my blooming, blushing bride
She looked so nice I had to start canoodling
But she woke the whole hotel up when she cried

'That's a bloody silly place to put a banjo
You're a proper bloody fool to put it there
You can practise bloody daily
On your ukebloodylele
You can play Bill Bloody Bailey lad
And I don't care
You can hang your bloody banjo from the ceiling
You can stick it any other bloody where
But that's a bloody silly place to put a banjo
You're a proper bloody fool to put it there!'

PLAYTIME

Midnight in the playground
he was found
clinging to an ostrich
on the Sorry-Go-Round

THE FIVE DOORS

Open the large cardboard box
Tear out the glossy transparent plastic
And unpack The Five Doors

The Five Doors comprise a kind of set
Students must arrange The Five Doors in the correct order
They are about one quarter the size of real doors

The Five Doors are painted white
Each has four yellow panels and a brass handle
Everybody is fascinated by The Five Doors

Suddenly The Five Doors are in the news
The tabloids think they're super-sexy
The broadsheets worry about their meaning

The Five Doors have their own TV show
It's on every night and repeated in the mornings
Mothers and babies and civil servants and junkies
They all smile the same smile
As they sit and watch The Five Doors

They do not open they do not close
They simply stand in the correct order
As the lights come up on them
And the lights shine brightly on them
And the lights fade away
And it is Goodnight to The Five Doors

One year later
The Ghosted Autobiography
Appears in the shops
Now the public knows the names
Of The Five Doors:

Knockerloose, Creaky, Warps, Ajar and Slammer
Now we know and the mystery's gone
Fuck The Five Doors – what's next?

three badly drawn chimpanzees
sitting on the glowing floorboards
of a long and empty attic
lit by a triangular window

it is the early 1930s
the chimps are advertising
Somebody's Floor Polish
the advert sways my heart

after searching
the mystery backstreets of the city
I stumble into a floor polish shop

I ask for a tin of Three Chimpanzees
the soap-faced shop-owner
stares at me silently
until I back out empty-handed

limping away down the cobbled street,
I can hear squeaky giggles
from a high triangular window

maybe they know I don't have a floor

MUCUS MEMBRANE'S TV SPECIAL

A montage of Mucus chatshow highlights
Watched by an audience of guffawing celebrity friends
But this is the Beard Special
So they all wear beards.
Then, down the Silver Staircase of the Stars
Prowls Mucus Membrane himself
Wearing a low-cut Highland gown by the Scab Sisters
And – guess what? – a sporran with a beard.

After the Presentation

Sir Mucus is escorted "backstage" at the Palace.
There he meets Prince Gullet, the sports car collector.
They discuss the roadholding merits
Of the 77B Slasher.
Princess Glug of Mercia leads Sir Mucus to the bar,
Puts down both her dry Martinis,
Gropes his velvet crotch
And collapses in mock hysteria.
The Duke of Rockall mistakes him for a waiter
Which appeals to the famous Mucus sense of humour.
Sir Mucus, a silver tray of champers balanced on his palm,
Prances up to Lord Ballord the bald tycoon
And asks if there is anything at all
That he can do for him.
Lord Ballord stares at him: 'Suck yourself off.'

The BRIGHT BOOK

they gave me a book
of beautiful paintings
with scarlet leather binding
and a golden clasp

they warned me:
as you turn the pages
the pictures become brighter
and brighter until they become

as bright as the sun
and brighter
anyone who reads to the end
will be stone blind

how did the painters
make the bright book?
they wore blindfolds
and double-dark goggles

and worked underground
in a black studio
by the light
of their own paintings

EPITIPE

new word invented by Brian Lawrence of Bradford to mean a palindrome, because he has always thought that a palindrome should itself be a palindrome. Now, how do I go about getting this accepted as a new word in the English language?

He can send it in to the Oxford English Dictionary, citing the fact that the word was used with this meaning in the following poem by Adrian Mitchell, the Shadow Poet Laureate on 29 September 2004:

LADY PALINDROME AT WORK

Madam likes sweet peas,
They're such a pretty pea.
She tends them in her garden
While composing an epitipe.

TELL ME LIES
OR TRUTH-ACHE IN THE
ANGLO-AMERICAN EMPIRE

122

AT THE CROSSROADS . . . .

I built the best of England
With my brain and with my hands.
Liberty Equality Fraternity –
That's where I took my stand,
And the people called me Old Labour
The brave heart of this land

I walked out of the smoky streets
To enjoy some country air,
But when I came to the crossroads,
I saw a weird sight there –
A man in a silver business suit
Swivelling in a black leather chair

He jumped right up and shook my hand
And giggled with mysterious glee.
Then he stared and said: 'Old Labour,
I can tell your destiny.
I'm the Great Political Entrepreneur –
Would you like to do a deal with me?'

Well, the style of his smile and the size of his eyes
Made him look like a shopping mall.
I told him straight: 'I'm a socialist,
I support fair shares for all.
He said: 'Capitalism *means* fair shares,
Provided that you play ball.'

I said: 'I can think of something
Capitalism can't arrange
And that's the common ownership
Of the means of production, distribution and exchange.
And war makes so much more profit
That the idea of peace is strange.

'I was born for peace and justice
For every race and nationality
I'm for people, not for profit,
I want to see the children free
With no more than twelve kids in a class
Revelling in liberty.'

'But let's not talk about the people,'
The sophisticated stranger said.
'You must have targets of your own –
Let's talk about you instead.'
And my brain was enthralled by his silver voice
Though my heart was filled with dread.

'I know you have a heart,' said the shining voice
'And I know you have an excellent mind.
Why not become an Entrepreneur –
Leave those people of yours behind?
You shall live in mansions and grand hotels
And be constantly wined and dined.

'You shall have your own island and bodyguard
And your own show on TV,
And a heated pool and a gymnasium
And become a powerful Celebrity.'
'I think I could fancy that,' I said,
But what's the cost going to be?'

Well, I knew. But I signed – in my own life-blood.
He extracted my soul with care
And placed it in his credit card case
And gave me his black leather chair
Then he laughed and said: 'You are New Labour now.'
I said: 'Thank you, Mr Blair.'

WHO CUT IT?

After the kindly surgeon
amputated all its limbs
Blinded it, pierced its eardrums,
and removed its brain and heart,

Who cut the throat of the Labour Party?
It cut its own stupid throat.

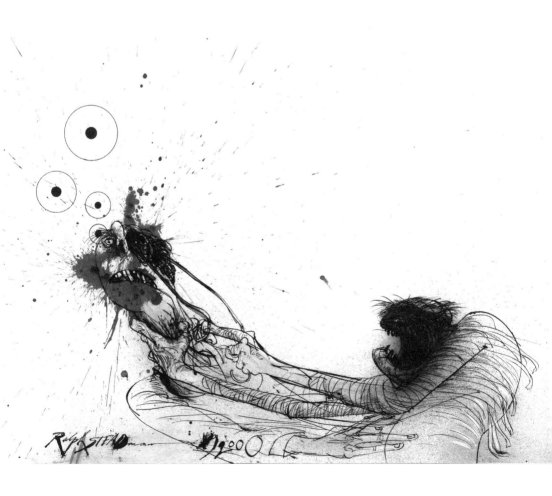

PEACETIME HAIKU

Try one hundred years
Without any wars at all –
Let's see if it works!

PEACE WORKS

The Doorbell

I was in bed, the silvery light of dawn
blessing our quiet suburban street,
when the window darkened,
and the doorbell rang.

Pushed my face deep in the pillow.
but the doorbell kept ringing
and there was another sound,
like the crying of a siren,
so I slopped downstairs
unbolted, unlocked, unchained
and opened the front door.

There, on the doorstep, stood the War.
It filled my front garden,
filled the entire street
and blotted out the sky.
It was human and monstrous,
shapeless, enormous,
with torn and poisoned skin which bled
streams of yellow, red and black.

The War had many millions of heads
both dead and half-alive,
some moaning, some screaming,
some whispering,
in every language known on earth,
goodbye, my love.

The War had many millions of eyes
and all wept tears of molten steel.
Then the War spoke to me
in a voice of bombs and gunfire:
I am your War.
Can I come in?

Dust and Ashes

The Cedars of Lebanon have been stripped of their bark,
cut down to the sap, hacked down to the roots.
Now they are ashes floating over blackened villages.

Israel has locked herself in the bathroom
and is slowly cutting her own throat.

England is hunting down insurgents in Iraq
and terrorists in London,
While selling weapons to anyone who wants to kill.

The USA arms the world at an enormous profit
under the trading name of Shock and Awe.
Washington is the new Rome
whose rulers plan the domination of the world.

What if the weird Barbarians resist?
Bomb them to dust and ashes.
Before we're through
the whole world of Aliens
will become a desert.

Yes the buildings, the cedars, the animals
and the people will be one dust storm,
a nuclear dust storm swirling round the world..

And when all the men and women and children are dead
in Dubai, Chicago, Beijing, Sydney, Rio de Janeiro and Paris –
when they are all dead
and all the animals
and all the trees
and all the birds
and all the insects –
their ashes will fly in their hot agony
and descend upon the waters,
and the poison ashes will murder the oceans
and all life will be wiped out –
    goodbye, my love.

tHE QUESTION

a favourite pond on Hampstead Heath.
a village in Lebanon, after an air raid.

       peace or global suicide?
          you decide.

watching over the pond, a wise heron.
in the village, a crushed house.

       peace or global suicide?
          you decide.

the heron takes flight as three dogs splash into the pond.
in the ruins of the house, a rescue party.

       peace or global suicide?
          you decide.

three dogs gallop out of the pond.
one of the rescue party shouts, Come here!

       peace or global suicide?
          you decide.

the dogs shake themselves and all the children laugh.
like a midwife, the rescuer draws a baby out of a heap of dust.

       peace or global suicide?
          you decide.

children and dogs scamper over the Heath.
the baby is covered with cement dust.

       peace or global suicide?
          you decide.

Is it all right to kill people?

I was watching the war
with my Mum and my Dad.
I said: is it all right to kill people?

Dad said: *If you're a soldier in a war*
it's OK to kill enemy soldiers
otherwise they'll kill you.

Is that the only time it's right to kill?

Well if a burglar broke in
and held a knife to Mum's throat –
it would be OK to kill him

How would I kill him?

Well, if you had a gun
you could shoot him.

I might hit Mum.

You could edge round from behind her
and shoot the burglar.

Can I have a gun?

No.

Then what am I supposed to do about Mum?

You'd better sneak out and phone 999.

Is it OK to kill a maths teacher?

Only if he's going to kill you.

I think my maths teacher
is trying to kill me
very gradually with maths.

Why do enemy soldiers want to kill us?

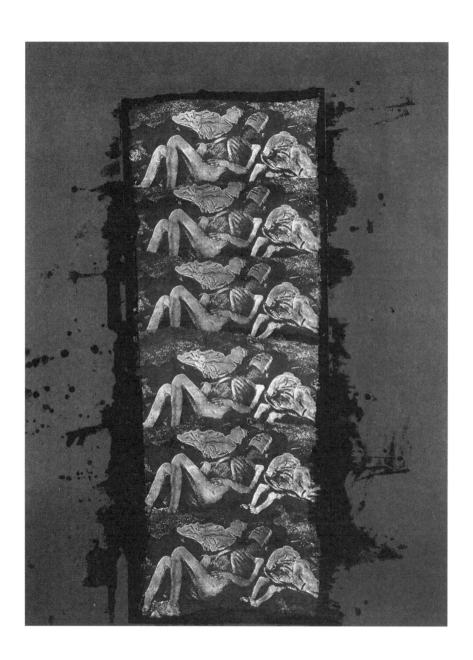

Because they've been taught
we want to kill them.
So they want to kill us first.

So are you teaching me
they want to kill me
so I'll want to kill them first?

Listen, son.
You're not the kind who ever learns
to clean and load and fire a gun.

What kind am I, Dad?

You're the kind who asks questions.
You're the kind who gets killed.

SUGGESTION

Each of the people killed on the road
Should be buried under a road hump.
Goodbye my darlings –
Bump bump bump.

PEACE AND PANCAKES

(A song, with music by Andrew Dickson, from the epic play, The Fear Brigade, first performed at the Global Village, near Maidstone, Kent, on 7 August 2006 to 5000 international young people. The play was commissioned by the Woodcraft Folk.)

the old world began
with a big bang
a big bang, a big bang

the new world begins
with a big song
a big song, a big song

it's got a strong beat
like your heartbeat
so use your two feet
to stomp out the beat

of a big song
of pancakes and peace
of a big song
everybody sing along

everybody loves pancakes
and everybody loves peace
you can find pancakes all round the world
north south west and east

dosas for breakfast in India
with spicy veg in the middle
Canadian maple syrup
on buckwheat cakes hot off the griddle
long live peace and pancakes!

the Greeks make pancakes with semolina
Russians make their blinis with yeast
red-hot quesidillas in Mexico City
yes pancakes turn any meal into a feast
long live peace and pancakes!

in Beijing they fill pancakes
with plum sauce and roast duck
every Shrove Tuesday in England
my pancake always gets stuck
            bad luck!
long live peace and pancakes!

the Koreans call their pancakes pa'chon
and cook 'em with sesame seeds
the Romans serve cannelloni
pancakes are the banquet everyone needs
long live peace and pancakes!

South Africa's banana chapatis
Brittany's crêpes suzettes
every woman and man from Chile to Japan
they're eating all they can get

everybody loves pancakes
and everybody loves peace
you can find pancakes all round the world
north south west and east

long live the planet earth
long live the animals
long live the birds and fishes
long live the forests and the oceans

long live the man
long live the woman
who use both courage and compassion
long live their children

long live peace
long live peace
long live peace and pancakes

TIGERS AND MONKEYS.

(for the Campaign Against the Arms Trade)

A tiger, trying to hunt a herd of deer
is followed through the woods
by hooting monkeys in the trees,
    who warn the deer:
  There's a killer coming –
Long live the monkeys!

PRINCE HARRY IN AFGHANISTAN....

what did it say on Prince Harry's hat?

WE DO BAD THINGS
TO BAD PEOPLE

yes I remember Jesus saying that.

THE WAR ON TERROR
CHAPTER 13

Prince Harry is home from Afghanistan.
He flew out a Twerp, but he flies back a Man.
Do you feel safer now he is back?
Or should all of the Royals be sent to Iraq?

The Song of the Great Crack

(On a visit to Tate Modern I was fascinated by Shibboleth, the Great Crack in the floor of the Turbine Hall, the work of the Colombian artist Doris Salcedo. When I was asked by the BBC radio drama series, Fact For Fiction, to write a topical play, I chose to centre it around the Crack.)

(The commission was to write an eleven minute play to be discussed on Monday, written on Tuesday, rewritten on Wednesday, rehearsed on Thursday, recorded on Friday and transmitted on Saturday and Sunday. I took on the assignment on condition I could work with my old mate Andy Roberts – singer, guitarist, composer and adventurer. We played both the parts in this play, from which this spoken song is taken and freely adapted.)

I'm standing, rather unsteadily,
in the the gigantic Turbine Hall
of the Tate Modern;
staring down the silky smooth cement floor
as it slopes slowly downhill.
I gaze down the length
of the great crack in the floor
cutting its dark and zigzag way
down and down to the hall's far end –
to disappear under a set of green glass doors.
Something snaps in my memory:
I've been here before.

the crack seems like an open wound
with stitches of steel all along its dark sides

   it's the great crack
like a jagged version of a dried-up Mississippi
     the great crack
a gigantic lightning stroke right down the floor

for the great crack in the floor of the turbine hall
     is all the grief of the world

and the great crack is the opening to
the underworld of western civilisation
and to the many convoluted hells
of the Third World and the Fourth World

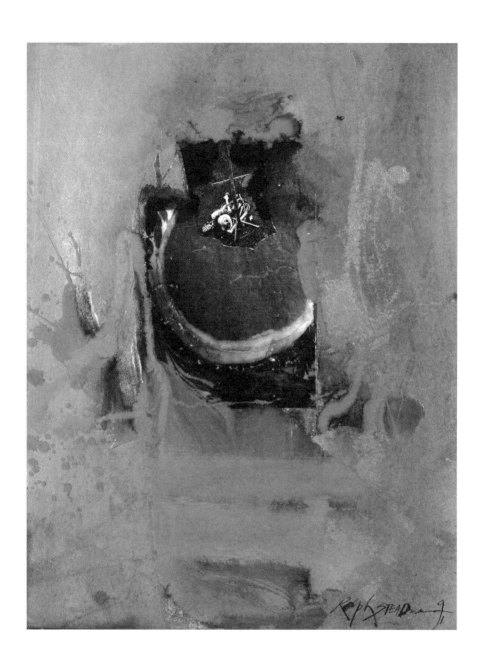

and the great crack in the floor
is the grinning mouth
of the shaking world
as it laughs like an earthquake
at the follies of the human race

and the great crack is a map
of the painful progress of their history

and the great crack is a trap
for boobies
WARNING please watch your step

and the great crack is the wrong end of the stick
which I always clasp so fervently

and the great crack
is an advertisement
for the British arms trade
the third biggest in the world
as it stands on its podium spraying blood champagne
just below the USA and Russia

and the great crack
is Lethe the river of forgetfulness
which the mass media drinks each night
to wash away the past

and the great crack
is the cry of the massacred innocents
poor hungry raped or murdered

and the great crack
is the handwriting of an alien
whose love letter to the human race says:
mene mene tekel upharsin
you have been weighed in the balance
and found wanting

and the great crack
is despair
that useless emotion
which sometimes threatens
to flood the mind

and the great crack
is the trumpet of Louis Armstrong
breaking open the sun itself

and the great crack
is the life of Anne Frank
and the song of Aretha Franklin

the great crack
is the crooked trench
down which all the dead of World War One
are slowly walking homewards –
   leave your backdoor open for Tommy

and the great crack
is not the straight and narrow way of the righteous
but the dark mazy pathway of our children

and the great crack
is the cry of the extinct animals

and the great crack
is the black hole in the universe
towards which we are travelling
too fast for my liking

and the great crack
is a refuge for insects
and a channel
for the tears of mourners

and the great crack
is the mark of Captain Ahab
and the revenge of Moby-Dick

and the great crack
is the mind of King Lear
with his dead darling in his arms.

and the great crack
is the thunderstroke of Zeus

and the great crack
is the tag of the Graffiti Cassandra
announcing the end of the world

145

and the great crack
is an advertisement for cancer

and the great crack
is the jab of heroin
the murderer who took my extra daughter

and the great crack
is the heart of the heartless world

and the great crack
is the second coming of Spike Milligan
with the daft joke that would save the human race

and the great crack
is a souvenir of Hiroshima
and an early warning
of the nuclear war
which will crack the world apart

and the great crack
is the Mersey river
carrying a riverboat full
of rock and poetry

The great crack
is the onstage death
of Tommy Cooper

the great crack
is the bicycle track of the late magician
Ivor Cutler

the great crack
is the mark of the ice skate
on which Long John Silver
sped down the Glacier of Doom

the great crack, says Doctor Watson,
must be a clue

the great crack
is the last laugh
and the famous last word
and the crack of doom
and the lost chord

the great crack
is the truth about Father Christmas
and the soul of the Labour Party

the great crack
is the cry of monks
shot by soldiers in Rangoon
and the cry of demonstrators
shot by soldiers in Derry

the great crack
is where we put criminals
we don't know what to do with
and old people and children and mad people
we don't know what to do with
the official title for this facility is:
The Ignorance Institute.
We put them there and ignore them.
It is best to ignore the Ignorance Institute

the great crack
is the poetry of the forgotten

the great crack
is Ralph Steadman's attempt at a straight line
and the great crack
is Leonardo Da Vinci's attempt
at a Ralph Steadman drawing.

and the great crack
is Desmond Tutu crying to the deaf world
for an end to all executions

and all the time the great crack is –
as its creator Doris Salcedo of Colombia says –
the war between the rich and the poor.

and suddenly I know where I saw it before
the great crack in the turbine hall floor
is the lightning shock
that divided me one night
from my skull down to my bare feet
with a shining zigzag
which burned white-hot
but did not hurt at all
as I stood clinging on
to the bathroom basin for balance

and dear life
stricken maybe by age or grief

so that for ten seconds or maybe twelve
the only live thing in the dark still world
was that white crack down the middle of my being
that great crack

And the great crack sings
in the voice of Paul Robeson
blessed are they that mourn
for they are not dead
blessed are the peacemakers
for their grandchildren will love them

So can the great crack ever be healed?
Only by the return of the Sultan's Elephant
and the Little Giant Girl
from the Space Rocket.

For I went with my wife
and grand-daughter to the Mall
where we danced
to the Sultan's Elephant
and fell in love with
the Little Giant Girl
and all the great city of London rejoiced.

Small Boy Sprains Ankle In Great Crack
Wow! Health and Safety! Action!!

Last year more than a hundred people
tripped or slipped on the hills of Hampstead Heath, maybe
distracted from where they were putting their feet
by a celestial sky or love or Keats or maybe rain.
More than a hundred injured ankles and wrists.
Wow! Health and Safety! Action!!!

We have now cemented over
the hills and dales and woods and ponds
of Hampstead Heath –
all except for one Great Crack.

To Whom It May Concern Remix

Come all ye –
   wartbrain psychics
  with asteroid sidekicks
    prostate agents
    and plastic Cajuns

    royal doggerellas
  cluster bombsellers
   alternative surgeons
    torturesport virgins

heavy vivisectionists
columnists, Golumnists,
priests of the beast
who are secretly policed
by highranker bankers
playing pranks with tankers

ghost advisers
death advertisers
vampire preachers
sucked-dry teachers
beheaded dead bodies
of blank-hearted squaddies

billionaire beauticians
fishing for positions
from poison politicians
with obliteration missions –
I'm alone, I'm afraid
And I need your aid
   can't you see – can't you see – can't you see?

I was run over by the truth one day
Ever since the accident I've walked this way
    So stick my legs in plaster
    Tell me lies about Vietnam

Heard the alarm clock screaming with pain
Couldn't find myself, so I went back to sleep again
    So fill my ears with silver
    Stick my legs in plaster
    Tell me lies about Vietnam

Every time I shut my eyes, all I see is flames
I made a marble phone-book, and I carved all the names
    So coat my eyes with butter
    Fill my ears with silver
  Stick my legs in plaster
    Tell me lies about Vietnam

I smell something burning, hope it's just my brains
They're only dropping peppermints and daisy-chains
    So stuff my nose with garlic
    Coat my eyes with butter
    Fill my ears with silver
  Stick my legs in plaster
    Tell me lies about Vietnam

Where were you at the time of the crime?
Down by the Cenotaph, drinking slime
    So chain my tongue with whisky
    Stuff my nose with garlic
    Coat my eyes with butter
    Fill my ears with silver
  Stick my legs in plaster
    Tell me lies about Vietnam

You put your bombers in, you put your conscience out
You take the human being, and you twist it all about
    So scrub my skin with women
    So chain my tongue with whisky
    Stuff my nose with garlic
    Coat my eyes with butter
    Fill my ears with silver
  Stick my legs in plaster
    Tell me lies about –
Iraq
Burma
Afghanistan
BAE Systems
Israel
Iran

Tell me lies Mr Bush
Tell me lies Mr Blairbrowncameron

Tell me lies about Vietnam

LEAR + HIS FOOL   Ralph STEADman

WORK BY ADRIAN MITCHELL

POETRY
Greatest Hits: His 40 Golden Greats (Bloodaxe Books, 1991).
Blue Coffee: Poems 1985-1996 (Bloodaxe Books, 1996).
Heart on the Left: Poems 1953-1984 (Bloodaxe Books, 1997).
All Shook Up: Poems 1997-2000 (Bloodaxe Books, 2000).
The Shadow Knows: Poems 2000-2004 (Bloodaxe Books, 2004).
Tell Me Lies: Poems 2005-2008 (Bloodaxe Books, 2009).

POETRY FOR CHILDREN
The Orchard Book of Poems (Orchard, 1993).
Dancing in the Street (Orchard, 1999).
Umpteen Pockets: Collected Poems for Children (Orchard, 2009).
Shapeshifters: poems from Ovid's Metamorphoses (Frances Lincoln, 2009).

PLAYS
The Pied Piper (Oberon Books).
Gogol: The Government Inspector (Methuen).
Calderon: The Mayor of Zalamea and two other plays (Absolute Classics, Oberon).
*Lope de Vega: Fuente Ovejuna and Lost in a Mirror (*Absolute Classics, Oberon).
Tyger Two, Man Friday, Satie Day/Night and In the Unlikely Event of an Emergency (Oberon Books).
The Siege (Oberon Books).
The Mammoth Sails Tonight! (Oberon Books).
The Snow Queen (Oberon Books).
The Lion, the Witch and the Wardrobe (Oberon Books).
Alice in Wonderland and Through the Looking Glass (Oberon Books).
Two Beatrix Potter Plays: Jemima Puddleduck and Her Friends and Peter Rabbit and His Friends (Oberon Books).

CHILDREN'S STORIES
The Ugly Duckling (Dorling Kindersley).
The Steadfast Tin Soldier (Dorling Kindersley).
Maudie and the Green Children (Tradewind).
Nobody Rides The Unicorn (Transworld).
My Cat Mrs Christmas (Orion).
The Adventures of Robin Hood and Marian (Orchard Books).

RECORDINGS
The Dogfather: double CD (57 Productions).
Adrian Mitchell reading from his poems (The Poetry Archive).

For more information, check out www.adrianmitchell.co.uk
To obtain copies of these or out of print books by Adrian Mitchell, contact
Ripping Yarns Bookshop at 335 Archway Road, London N6 4EJ or by e-mail
at yarns@rippingyarns.co.uk.